Scary Creatures OF THE SOIL

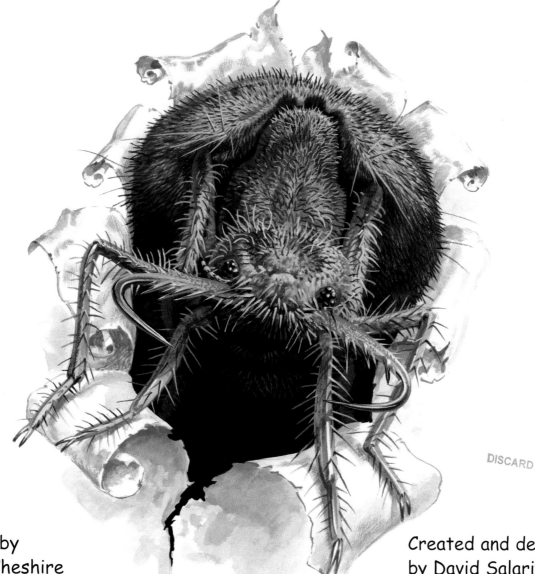

Written by
Gerard Cheshire

Created and designed
by David Salariya

Franklin Watts®
An Imprint of Scholastic Inc.
NEW YORK • TORONTO • LONDON • AUCKLAND • SYDNEY
MEXICO CITY • NEW DELHI • HONG KONG
DANBURY, CONNECTICUT

Author:

Gerard Cheshire has written many
books on natural history, and over the past
twelve years has cultivated an excellent
reputation as an author and editor. He now lives
in Bath, England, with his wife and three sons.

Artists:
David Antram
Janet Baker and Julian Baker
   (JB Illustrations)
Mark Bergin
Robert Morton
Bob Moulder
Carolyn Scrace

Series Creator: 20.66
                4.13

David Salariya was born in Dundee,
Scotland. He established The Salariya Book Company
in 1989. He has illustrated a wide range of books and
has created many new series for publishers in the UK
and overseas. He lives in Brighton, England, with his
wife, illustrator Shirley Willis, and their son.

Editorial Assistants:
Rob Walker, Tanya Kant

Picture Research:
Mark Bergin, Carolyn Franklin

Photo Credits:

Dreamstime: 9, 16, 21, 22
Fotolia: 5, 6, 8, 25, 26
Jonathan Salariya: 18
iStockphoto: 10, 11, 12, 27
United States Department of Agriculture: 19

Created, designed, and produced by
The Salariya Book Company Ltd
25 Marlborough Place, Brighton BN1 1UB

A CIP catalog record for this title is available
from the Library of Congress.

ISBN-13: 978-0-531-21821-1 (Lib. Bdg.)
         978-0-531-22226-3 (Pbk.)
ISBN-10: 0-531-21821-X (Lib. Bdg.)
         0-531-22226-8 (Pbk.)

Published in 2009 in the United States by
Franklin Watts
An Imprint of Scholastic Inc.
557 Broadway
New York, NY 10012

Printed in China

Termite mound

PAPER FROM
SUSTAINABLE
FORESTS

Contents

Giant anteater

Can Beetles Bury the Dead?

When you step on soil, you are stepping on a creature's **habitat**. Many animals live in the soil, including burying beetles.

Burying beetles are a type of **insect** that can bury animal bodies. First, they find a **carcass**. Then, they dig away the soil underneath, until the body is hidden in the ground. The female lays eggs very close to the carcass. Then, when the **larvae** hatch, they have their own private food supply.

Did You Know?

Some burying beetles are brightly colored. They also taste unpleasant. **Predators** learn to avoid beetles with these colors.

Wolf spider

Burying beetles

Burying beetles use their strong legs to dig away the soil underneath dead **mammals** and birds.

Dead blue jay

Stag beetle

Mandible

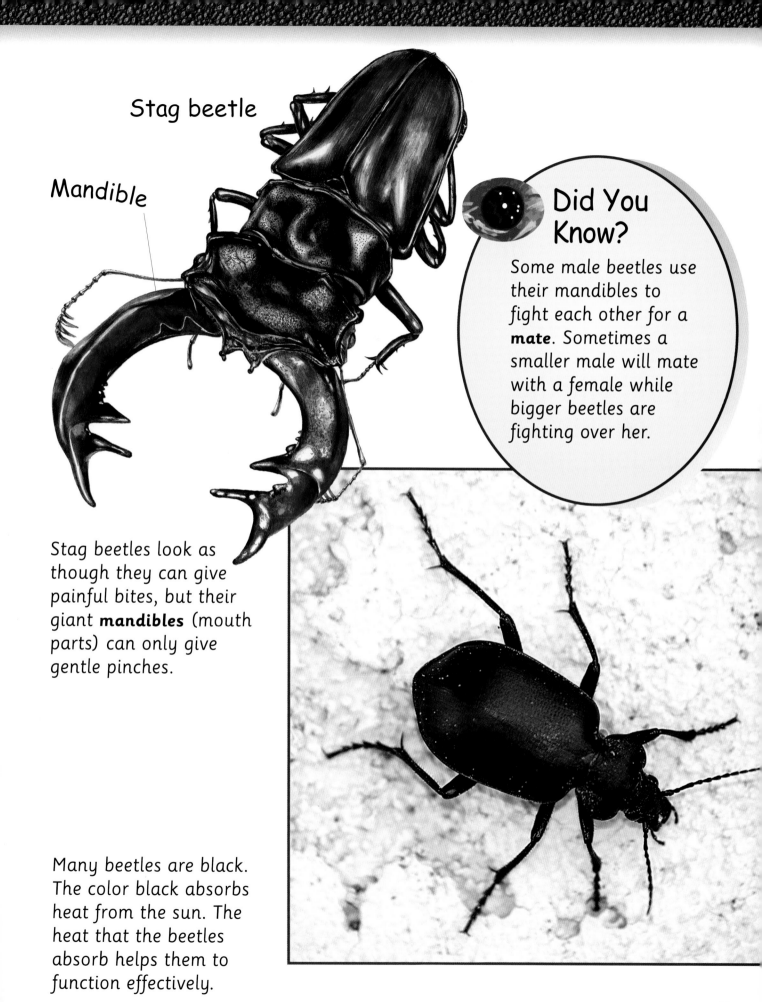

Did You Know?

Some male beetles use their mandibles to fight each other for a **mate**. Sometimes a smaller male will mate with a female while bigger beetles are fighting over her.

Stag beetles look as though they can give painful bites, but their giant **mandibles** (mouth parts) can only give gentle pinches.

Many beetles are black. The color black absorbs heat from the sun. The heat that the beetles absorb helps them to function effectively.

How Do Spiders Ambush Their Prey?

All spiders are predators. They catch other animals and feed on them by secreting a special fluid that turns the **prey** into mush. Many spiders use webs to catch their prey, but some spiders use different methods. Wolf spiders hunt by chasing down and grabbing their prey. Trap-door spiders snatch their prey from below. Woodlouse spiders hunt at night and poison their prey.

A tangled web to trap insects

Orb spiders make neat spiraling webs to catch flying insects. Funnel-web spiders make funnel-shaped webs on the ground to catch walking insects. Some types of spiders make tangled webs to catch insects as they land.

Trap door   Twig trap

Centipede

Did You Know?
The trap-door spider has sensitive hairs on its front two pairs of legs. These hairs detect vibrations made by passing animals. This is how the spider knows when its prey is near.

Silk lining

Trap-door spiders use a trap door, made from silky strands of web, to catch prey and to hide from predators. The trap door is so well hidden that insects and other small animals walk over it, and then the spider grabs them through the webbing. Some trap-door spiders have a hidden chamber at the bottom of their **burrow**. The spider hides in the chamber when predatory centipedes enter its burrow.

Hidden chamber

Trap-door spider

Trap-door spider

Trap-door spider
Trap-door spiders have special mouth parts that they use to dig their burrows.

What Feeds Poop to Its Babies?

Dung beetles feed on animal dung (or poop). Some simply lay their eggs on dung, and their larvae burrow inside. Others, like certain types of scarab beetles, roll dung into balls, and then bury them along with their larvae. Burying the dung protects their young from predators such as birds, and hides the dung from other hungry animals.

Scarab beetles have spiky front legs, which they use to shape and bury the balls of dung.

Spiky front leg

Scarab beetle

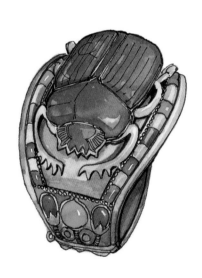

Egyptian ring

The ancient Egyptians worshipped scarab beetles. They believed that a giant scarab rolled the sun across the sky, just as beetles roll balls of dung. Khepri was the name of the Egyptian scarab god.

Did You Know?

The name "scarab" comes from the Latin word *scarabaeus*, which means "beetle."

Dung beetles

Usually the male rolls the dung ball with his hind legs, but sometimes male and female beetles work together.

How Can Owls Nest Where There Are No Trees?

When there are no trees for building nests, most birds just have to nest on the ground. This is dangerous because it is easy for predators to find these nests and eat the eggs and chicks inside them. The burrowing owl nests *under* the ground instead. It uses burrows that have been abandoned by rabbits or other animals.

The burrowing owl has long legs and large feet. It uses them to scrape loose soil and rocks out of abandoned burrows before making its nest.

A pair of burrowing owls on the ground outside the entrance to their nest hole

A burrowing owl sitting inside a hole made by a prairie dog

What Type of Insect Builds Cities Underground?

Some insects are described as **social insects**, because they live in vast **colonies** of hundreds or thousands that are almost like cities. Some social insects build their nests in the ground, where they are safe from predators and the temperature stays the same all year round. Ground-nesting social insects include ants, termites, bumblebees, and some types of wasps.

X-Ray Vision

Hold the next page up to the light and see what's inside a termite mound.

See what's inside

Termites

Termite nests are composed of many tunnels and chambers. The nests are made of mud that is a mixture of soil and termite spit. When the mud dries, it is very hard and strong.
Termites are sometimes called "white ants," but they are not closely related to real ants.

Termite mound

13

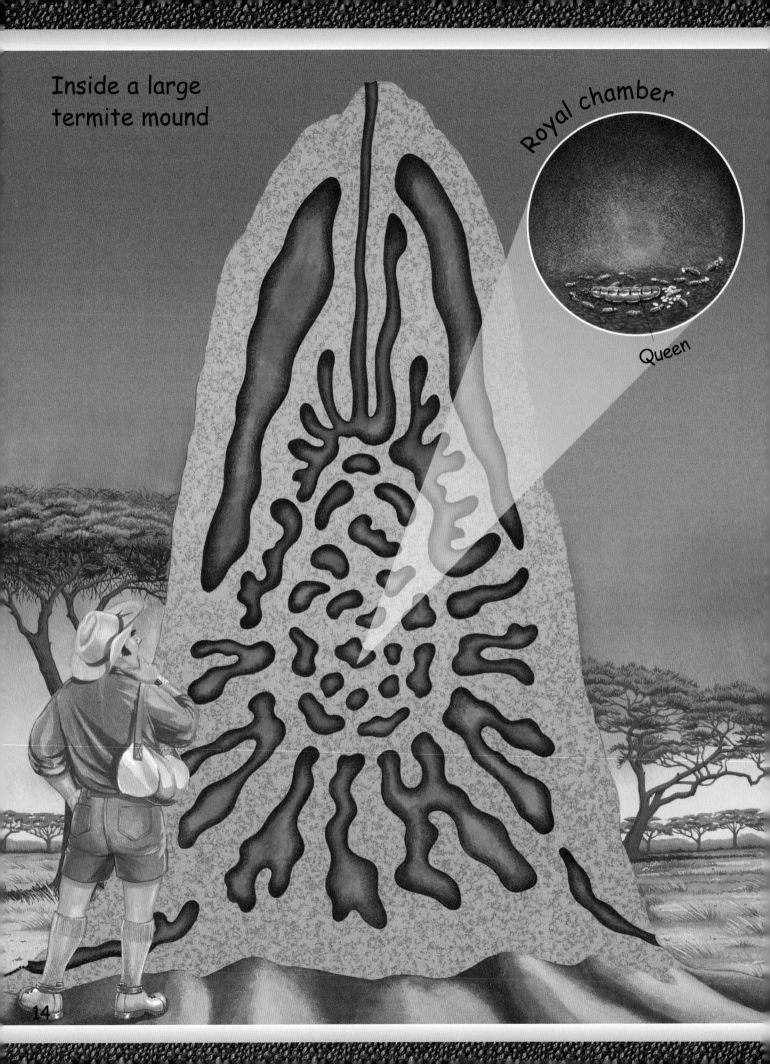

Inside a large
termite mound

Royal chamber

Queen

14

What's Inside a Termite Mound?

Deep in the center of the termite mound is the royal chamber, where the queen lives. Her job is to lay eggs so that there are always new termites to replace those that get eaten by predators. Although a queen is too large to move, she can produce anywhere from 2,000 to 30,000 eggs per day, depending on her **species**.

In some ways, a large termite mound is like a castle. It has chimneys and vents to keep the nest cool during the heat of the day.

Most of the termites in a colony are either workers or soldiers. Workers do all of the nest maintenance and attend to the **queen**. Soldiers defend the nest against predators.

Some male termites are called kings. They **fertilize** the queen so that her eggs can hatch into larvae.

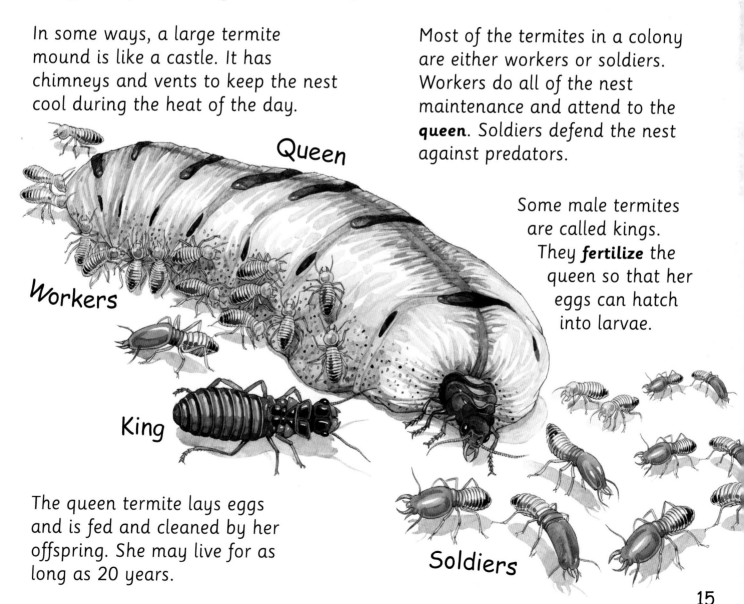

Queen

Workers

King

Soldiers

The queen termite lays eggs and is fed and cleaned by her offspring. She may live for as long as 20 years.

When Are Termites in Trouble?

Termites make a good meal for animals that can break into their nests. One expert termite eater is the giant anteater. It has enormous claws on its front feet that can rip holes in a termite mound. It also has a long snout, which it pokes inside the nest to feed on the termites. It uses its long, sticky tongue to lap up the insects by the thousands.

Giant anteater

Termite mound

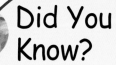

Did You Know?

Anteaters have no teeth. Like birds, they have a **gizzard**—a part of the stomach that contains small stones to grind up food after the anteater has swallowed it.

Aardvark

Long tongue

Sharp claws

Aardvarks emerge from their underground burrows in the late afternoon to **forage** for ants or termites. They scoop up termites with their 12-inch (30-cm) tongues.

Other termite-eaters include armadillos, pangolins, and echidnas. Like anteaters, they all have large claws to break into nests and long snouts to reach termites.

When the predators are finished eating, the termites repair their nest.

Worms

Worms eat rotted carcasses buried in the ground. As carcasses **decompose**, their **nutrients** are released into the soil and worms **recycle** them.

Why Are Worms Good for Soil?

Earthworms are very important for the soil. They create a network of tunnels that keep the soil well drained and **ventilated**. These tunnels help plants to grow. Worms also eat the pieces of animals and plants that have rotted into the soil. Their dung then enriches the soil, making it even better for plants.

What is a nematode worm?

Nematode worms are usually smaller than earthworms, and their bodies are not divided into segments (ring-like sections). Most nematodes are only 1 millimeter long, but they play a very important role in the decomposition and recycling of nutrients.

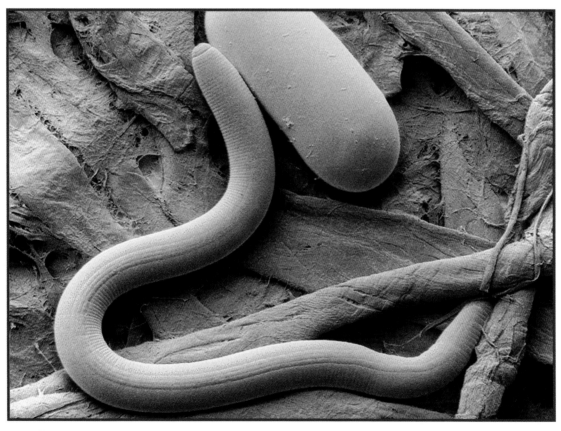

Nematode worm and its egg, viewed through a microscope

Can Lions Live in the Ground?

Of course, real lions don't live underground, but one insect is so scary that it is named after a lion! The adult antlion is a flying insect that looks like a dragonfly, but its larva is a predator of ants.

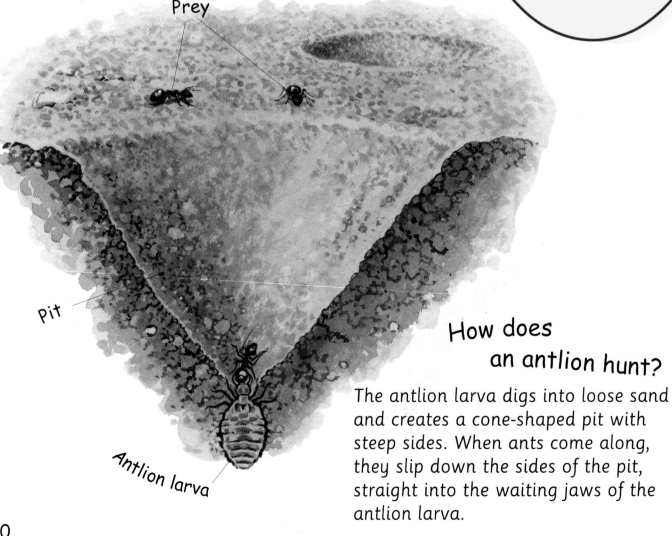

Prey

Pit

Antlion larva

How does an antlion hunt?

The antlion larva digs into loose sand and creates a cone-shaped pit with steep sides. When ants come along, they slip down the sides of the pit, straight into the waiting jaws of the antlion larva.

To humans, an antlion larva is small and harmless, but to an ant, it is a giant monster!

Antlion larva

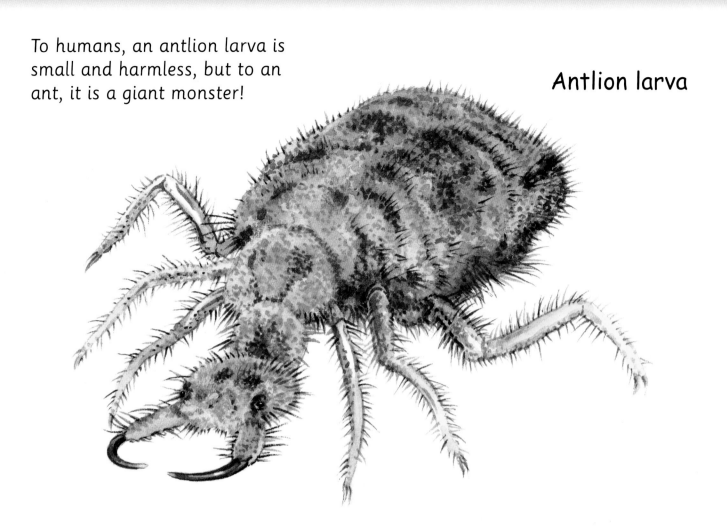

How does a larva become an adult?

When an antlion larva is fully grown, it goes through a process called **metamorphosis** and becomes a flying adult. It then goes off to find a mate.

Adult antlion

Are There Tiny Tigers?

Tiger beetles and their larvae are ferocious predators of other insects and **invertebrates**. The tiger beetle larva ambushes its prey by hiding in the ground and then pouncing on creatures that come too close. The adult beetle is very quick and **agile**. Its large, forward-facing eyes help it to spot its victims.

Did You Know?

If a tiger beetle were the same size as a human, it could run ten times faster than the fastest sprinter.

Tiger beetle

The tiger beetle uses its powerful jaws to grab and pierce its prey. Then it releases fluid that turns the prey into mush.

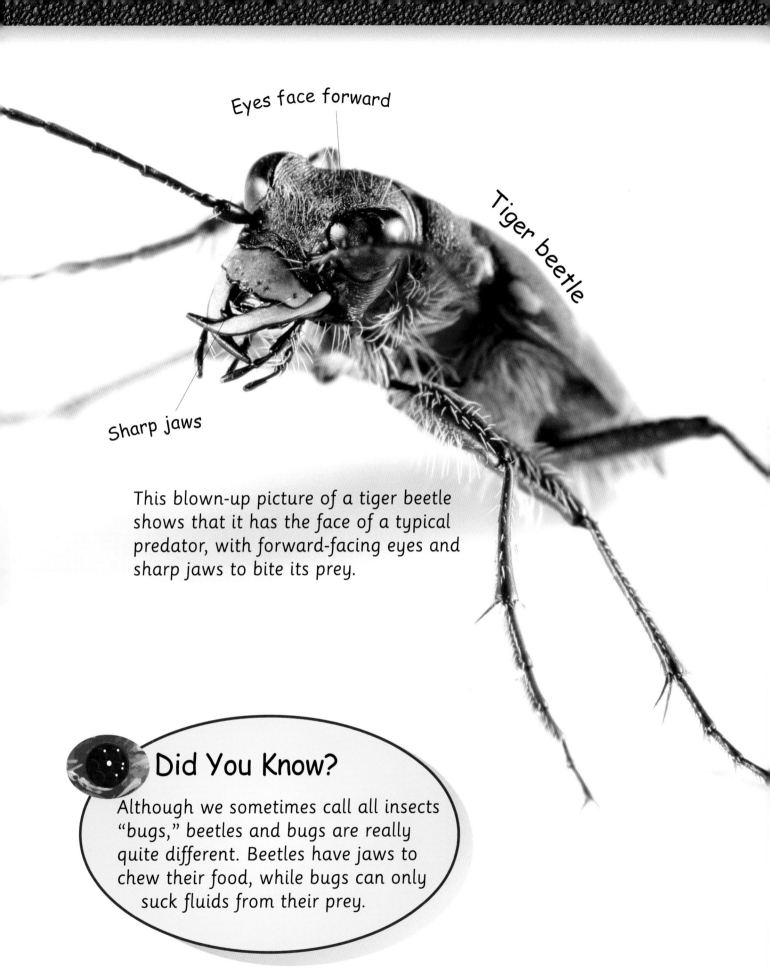

Eyes face forward

Tiger beetle

Sharp jaws

This blown-up picture of a tiger beetle shows that it has the face of a typical predator, with forward-facing eyes and sharp jaws to bite its prey.

Did You Know?

Although we sometimes call all insects "bugs," beetles and bugs are really quite different. Beetles have jaws to chew their food, while bugs can only suck fluids from their prey.

What Lives in a Hole?

There are many larger animals that live in holes in the ground. They include mammals, birds, and **reptiles**. Living below ground provides safety from predators and protection from the weather. Some animals also find their food under the ground.

X-Ray Vision

Hold the page opposite up to the light to see why these rabbits are hiding in their burrow.

See what's inside

Prairie dogs

Prairie dogs are not dogs, but **rodents**. They live in colonies and dig networks of tunnels.

Moles live and feed underground, eating worms and other invertebrates.

Mole

Weasel

How Safe Is a Burrow?

Predators such as weasels, polecats, ferrets, mink, and snakes have long, narrow bodies. They can easily enter the tunnels of animals that live underground. For this reason, many burrowing animals build escape tunnels so that they can get away if predators come looking for them.

Rattlesnake

Snakes are dangerous predators for animals below ground. They can slip silently into tunnels and quickly bite their prey before it has time to escape.

Weasel

A weasel's body is no wider than its head. If it can get its head inside a tunnel, it knows that its body will fit, too.

Did You Know?

A rattlesnake bites its prey and then follows the victim's scent trail until the poison kills it. Then the rattlesnake can easily swallow it.

Where Do These Scary Creatures Live?

Burrowing animals are found in almost every part of the world. This map shows where some of them live.

Burrowing owl

Some burrowing owls live in desert areas in North and South America, where there are no trees in which to nest.

Prairie dog

Prairie dogs, as their name suggests, inhabit the prairies of North America.

Rattlesnake

Rattlesnakes can be found in most of North America and parts of South America.

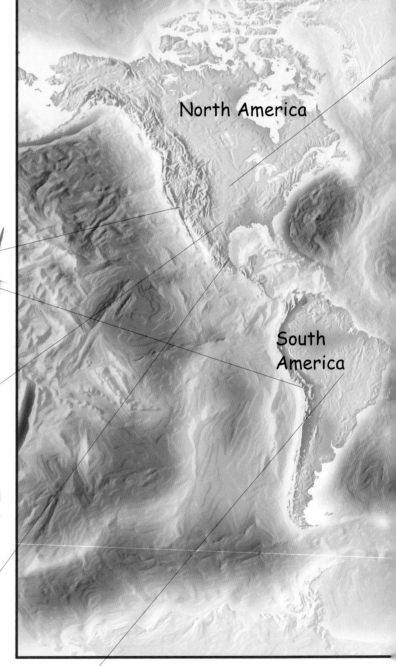

North America

South America

Giant anteater

Giant anteaters live in regions of South and Central America, where termites build their mounds.

Antlion larva

Antlions live in sandy places, where their larvae can build cone-shaped pits to trap ants.

Mole

Moles inhabit **temperate** places where the soil is easy to tunnel through and has plenty of worms.

Asia

Europe

Africa

Australia

Antarctica

Trap-door spider

Trap-door spiders are common in parts of Asia and Australia, where it is warm and fairly dry.

Termite

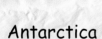

Termites inhabit warm places around the world, including Africa, Asia, the Americas, and Australia.

Scarab beetle

The scarab beetle was once worshipped in Egypt. It can be found all over the world.

Soil Facts

There are around 70,000 different types of soil in the United States alone.

Soil is formed by natural processes such as the wearing away of rocks by wind and rain. It takes hundreds of years for even a centimeter of soil to be formed in this way.

Up to one million earthworms can live in just one acre (0.4 hectare) of soil.

If an earthworm is cut or torn in two by a predator, the worm can sometimes regrow its missing end and live normally. But it's not true that both ends can grow to make two worms.

Termite mounds in the deserts of Australia have measured over 42 feet (13 m) high and 98 feet (30 m) around.

Mole mounds—the mounds of soil that moles leave behind as they dig—can be up to 2 feet (60 cm) tall.

A trap-door spider can live for up to 20 years. It usually stays in the same burrow, widening it as the spider grows.

Weasels are predators of many burrowing animals, such as rabbits. But weasels themselves fall prey to bigger animals such as foxes, hawks, and cats. Only about one weasel out of 80 lives longer than two years.

A burying beetle can completely bury a small animal carcass in about eight hours.

Giant anteaters are threatened by humans in two ways. They are hunted for sport, and their Central and South American habitats are being destroyed by human development.

European rabbits are very social animals and live in groups of about 20. They live in burrow systems known as warrens.

The larvae of American cicadas can remain hidden in the soil for 17 years before developing into adults.

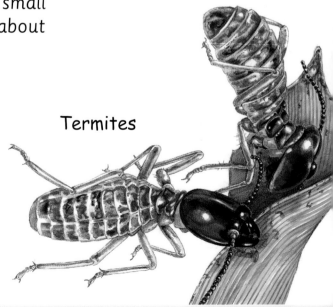

Termites

Glossary

agile Fast and flexible.

burrow (noun) A hole that an animal lives in.

carcass A dead body.

colony A large group of the same type of animal that lives together.

decompose To rot and break down into separate parts.

fertilize To combine egg and sperm to produce offspring.

forage To search for food.

gizzard In birds and some other animals, a part of the stomach that contains stones which grind up food.

habitat The natural home of a plant or an animal.

insect An invertebrate with six legs and a body made of three parts: head, thorax, and abdomen.

invertebrate An animal with no backbone.

larva (plural **larvae**) The young of an animal that will change into a different form when it becomes an adult.

mammal An animal that is born alive and then fed by its mother's milk.

mandibles Jaws or mouth parts, especially those of an insect.

mate (noun) A partner of the opposite sex; (verb) to join together to make offspring.

metamorphosis The process by which larvae change into adults.

nutrients The food or chemicals that a living thing needs in order to survive and grow.

predator An animal that kills and eats other animals.

prey An animal that is killed and eaten by a predator.

queen A female insect that lays eggs. In a colony of social insects, there is usually only one queen.

recycle To use a second time.

reptile A cold-blooded animal with scales.

rodent A mammal with gnawing teeth, such as a mouse or rat.

social insects Insects that live together in large colonies.

species A group of animals or plants that look the same, live in the same way, and can mate with each other to produce young.

temperate Neither very hot nor very cold.

ventilated Open to a current of fresh air.

Index

Mole